3 Days in Rome Trave

Rome (Image Credit, Nick Kenrick, Flickr/cc)

This is a **three days' guide to Rome**, with a perfect **72 hours' plan** that will guide you on the best way to enjoy this amazing city. We include all tips, maps, costs, and travel information so that you feel like you have your best friend with you showing you around Rome.

We developed this guide with the help of **local experts** and **travel bloggers** who live or frequently visit Rome so that you get only the best option on *where to stay*, where *to eat*, what monuments *to see*, how *to move around* Rome and how to enjoy this vibrant city at its best.

The **maps** provided can be accessible in their online format, at **Google maps**, which will enable you to navigate easily towards them while you are in Rome.

This guide is best enjoyed by **solo travelers** and **couples** or **groups of friends** traveling together to Rome. **Families** traveling with kids to Rome may also find a lot of useful details for planning their trip.

Have fun in Rome and thank you for choosing a Guidora guide!

Table of Contents

3 Days in Rome Travel Guide

Practical Information

Top Tips for Traveling to Rome

Where to Stay in Rome

How to Get from the Airport to the Center of Rome

Shopping in Rome

Our favorite Dining Place in Rome

1st Day In Rome - Itinerary

   1st Day in Rome - Map

   ZoomTip 1.1: Transportation in Rome

   ZoomTip 1.2: Information on the Monuments

2nd Day In Rome - Itinerary

   2nd Day in Rome – Map

   ZoomTip 2.1: Information on the Monuments

3d Day in Rome – Itinerary

   3d Day in Rome – Map

   ZoomTip 3.1: Information on the Monuments

Where to Eat in Rome

Where to Find the Best Ice Cream (Gelato) in Rome

Where to Find the Best Pizza in Rome

What Italian dishes to Try Except for Pizza and Pasta

Useful Italian Phrases

Thank You!

Copyright Notice

Practical Information

Average Airbnb price/night: 80 USD
Average Hotel Room price/night: 172 USD
Average Hostel Price/night: 28 USD
Sockets and Plugs: Italy uses 230V, 50Hz with the following socket types: C, F and L (different than UK's and US).

Weather: The warmest month is July with 89F (around 25 Celcius) and the coldest is January with 56F (around 8 Celcius)

Currency: Euro (1 Euro=1,15 USD)

Mc Meal at McDonald's: 8€
Meal in Inexpensive Restaurant: 17USD/15€
Meal in Mid-Range Restaurant for 2 people: 57USD/50€
One-way Ticket Local Transportation: 1.5€
Gasoline (1 Gallon): 5.6€
Cappuccino: 1.18€
Coca Cola: 2€
Water Bottle (1.5lt): 0.7€
Cigarettes (pack/Marlboro): 5.2€

Credit and Debit Cards: Visa, MasterCard, and Maestro are the most widely accepted. American Express is less common. Diners Club is pretty rare. Discover, JCB, UnionPay, and RuPay are unknown.

Tipping: Tipping is not usually expected in Rome. If you are happy with the service you may want to leave a tip (e.g. 5% of the bill). If the bill says that there is a "service charge" then the tip is included in the bill and you may not leave.

Mobile Phone: Italy uses GSM mobile network. You can buy a SIM card for about €7.69 ($8.79), which includes 3 GB of data plan. You can choose from 4 telecoms: 3 (Tre), Wind, Vodafone or Telecom Italia Mobile (TIM).

Dial Code: +39

Crime: Italy has the same crime rate with the United States of America, which is a medium risk rate.

Driving: Italians drive on the ride side of the road. Most cars have a manual transmission.

Speed Limits: 110 km/h (68 mph) on expressways, 130 km/h (80 mph) on motorways, 50-70 km/h (31-43 mph) in all built-up areas and 70-90 km/h (43-55 mph) on undivided highways

Driving License: International Driving Permit (IDP) is required alongside your original driving license.
Alcohol: It is legal to consume and buy alcohol above the age of 18 years old.

Drugs: Cannabis is illegal in Italy.

Emergency Numbers
Police: 112, Ambulance: 112, Fire Department: 112
Customs/Financial Police: 117
Official Language: Italian
Metric System: Kg, Cm/Mt/Km, Celcius

Top Tips for Traveling to Rome

#1 Be careful when you take a taxi from the airport: When you are at the airport, you will see a sign saying that a trip inside the Aurelian walls should cost 30 euros. However, many taxi drivers might tell you that the area you are going to is outside of the wall and will try to charge you with 40 or 50 euros. The taxi drivers do not speak English that well, so you may end up paying much more than you should. You could just take the express bus to Rome, which is around 6 euros per person. Take the Leonardo Express from Fiumicino which runs every half an hour or the Terravision shuttle service from Ciampino. You can also get the train, which costs 12 euros. If you decide to take a taxi, make sure that you have a clear understanding of the cost by asking the taxi driver.

#2 Stay away from the restaurants near the main tourist attractions if you want to taste some good food: We are biased towards the food in Rome. We believe that it is the worse you will find in Italy. The restaurants are hunting for tourists and do not offer the same quality as other places of Italy do. If you choose to eat in the restaurants near the main tourist attractions such as the Trevi Fountain, Spanish Steps, and Colosseum, you will most probably end up disappointed. Moreover, you should do your homework and learn about the four main pasta dishes you can eat in Rome: amatriciana, gricia, carbonara, cacio e Pepe.

#3 Buy your tickets online to save time from queueing: Rome has countless tourists, and there are often long lines at the main attractions. On the other side, these attractions have shorter lines for the visitors who have bought their tickets online. Online tickets are also cheaper than the ones you purchase on the front desk of the attractions. Just be careful that in some cases, e.g. in Colosseum, you have to print your online ticket and bring it with you – they cannot just scan your ticket on your smartphone.

#4 Try to Learn some basic Italian for Tourists: Italians in Rome do not communicate fluently in English, so it will be helpful if you also learn some phrases in Italian.

#5 Bring a comfortable pair of shoes with you: Rome is a vast area with many attractions, and you will do much walking. Bring some cute sneakers with you. However, Romans pay much attention to fashion, clothes, and shoes, and you should try to blend in. Especially, when you visit Cathedrals, you should take care of your attire, or you might not be allowed to enter. The signs at cathedrals inform visitors that women need to have their shoulders completely covered to be allowed to enter. This means that women should wear at minimum a t-shirt sleeve length. Moreover, the signs say that knees should be covered too for women. Of course, the Italian merchants, are inventive and resourceful, and you will often find vendors outside of the cathedrals, selling long scarfs to women who have forgotten about the dress code. Scarfs will do the job.

#6 Do not rent a car: Rome is a difficult city to drive through. Metro, taxis, and walking will help you get everywhere.

#7 You cannot hail taxis on the road. You can get them in taxi piazzas, or taxi queues which are scattered.

#8 Do not visit Rome during August. Everyone is on holidays. Most of the shops, bars, clubs, and theaters are closed. Yes, the attractions are still there to visit and see, but you will not get the real feeling of the town. Go in June or July if you need to be in Rome during the summer. April, May, September, and October are also great months to visit Rome as the weather is still warm.

#9 Keep your eyes open. Rome is among the top 5 cities in Europe to get pickpocketed. No matter if you are at the airport, or in the city center, always keep your eyes on your luggage and your stuff.

#10 Try to Fly to Ciampino and not Fiumicino Airport. The Ciampino airport hosts all the low-cost airlines, but the reason we recommend that you fly to Ciampino is that it will take you only 35-45 minutes to get to the center of Rome. If you fly to Fiumicino, you may need up to 90 minutes to reach the center of Rome.

#11 Do not get scammed. Do not let people give you roses on the Spanish Steps. You may think that it is for free, but it is not. Moreover, once you accept it, they will ask for money and will not accept it back. If you try to return the rose, you will see the whole gang coming at you and asking for money. Don't receive "presents" such as wristbands from strangers. They will come back asking for money, and you will lose 5 – 10 minutes trying to give the "presents" back to them.

#12 Try the Gelato. Rome may not have the best restaurants in Italy but serves the best ice-cream. Try as much Gelato as you can. In the touristic area, the best places to try the ice cream are **Il Palazzo del Freddo di Giovanni Fassi,** http://www.palazzodelfreddo.it/, **Giolitti,** (www.giolitti.it) **and** Il Geltone.

#13 Hop-on Hop-Off Bus: Some love them, some hate them. We don't like them to be honest, as we do prefer to walk around but if you are into this, you can get a ticket for 22 EUR per person per day, here.

Where to Stay in Rome

Our recommended hotel in Rome is *Hotel: Texas Hotel*
Address: Via Firenze 17, Rome
Tel.: (+39) 06 474 2107
Price/night: 95€ for a double room
Booking.com: Link
Recommended: Yes. Rome is expensive; and don't get us wrong; this is a budget solution and not some fancy 5-star hotel in Rome. But it will do its job. Comfortable rooms, friendly staff, located near the main attractions, low priced rooms compared to similar accommodations in Rome. Rome is a pretty expensive town to stay. Don't expect e.g. to find nice hotel rooms with 50-60 euros per night. On average, you should expect to pay at least 80 to 120 euros per night for a decent double room accommodation. The situation is almost the same if you try to book via Airbnb.

Photo: *Hotel Texas* **in Rome**

How to Get from the Airport to the Center of Rome

Rome has two airports. The **Fiumicino** airport and the **Ciampino** airport. Choose to fly to the Ciampino airport if you can, as it is closer to the center of Rome and it is cheaper to get from the airport to the center. Moreover, it is a smaller airport, and it is quicker to pass through security checks.

When you arrive at the Ciampino airport, there are three ways to get to the city center.

1. **Get a Taxi:** It will cost you at least 30 Euros. It is supposed to be a standard tariff. However, this is only for the hotels inside the walls of the city center. E.g., if you go close to Colosseum, it is not in the 30 euros standard tariff, and you may pay 45 or 50 euros. So, please make sure you ask the driver first about the total price before you jump into the taxi.
2. **Get a train.** We do not recommend it. The train station is 2kms away from the Ciampino airport, and you have to get a bus to go there. Then it takes 30 minutes to the Termini (the central station of Rome).
3. **Get a Bus.** There are three companies with buses, leaving from Ciampino airport. All three are excellent and punctual. The ticket costs 3.9 Euro per person. The drive takes 45 minutes from Ciampino to Termini, which is the central bus and rail station of Rome. Don't worry about timing; you will find at least one bus leaving every 30 minutes from Ciampino or Termini back to Ciampino:

Be aware that the Termini in Rome is not located in a beautiful area, as it seems quite scammy compared to the other parts of Rome. You should better not spend much time around there.

Shopping in Rome

Here are some tips about Shopping in Rome:
1. Don't expect to find great outlets with Prada, Gucci and other top brands inside Rome. There is a big one, but it is outside of Rome. The best time to get real bargains on premium brands is in February when the discounts in Rome take place in all the shops. Usually, they start at 50% off the regular prices.
2. The premium brands have their main shops in Piazza De Spagna. You will find Prada, Armani, Gucci, Bulgari and all other well-known brands there. The prices are high.
3. The best shop for men's fashion is "Boggi Milan." You can buy suits, shirts, shoes with fabulous Italian style. The prices are not that low though (e.g. a suit costs 600€, a pair of trousers costs 100€). It has several shops in Rome, e.g. at Via del Babuino, 20, 00187, which is 7 minutes' walk time from Piazza di Spagna.
4. If you want cheaper men's fashion, then you should go to a **Doppelganger** shop. Much lower prices but of course the quality and the fitting is not the same as the premium brands. Here you can find ties with 10-15€, suits, polos and other Italian fashion items.

The most interesting places for shopping in Rome are the following:

1. A.G.S Mercato Trionfale (1 Via La Goletta)
This is the oldest street market in Rome, which has been turned into an indoor market on 2009. You can find almost everything: fish, vegetables, honey, eggs, meat, etc.

2. Porta Portese Flea Market
This is the equivalent of Portobello market in London. Porta Portese flea market is the biggest and most famous flea market in Rome and it takes place every Sunday. It has thousands of stalls selling almost everything, new and old: bikes, shoes, clothes, electronics etc.

1 Porta Portese Market (credit)

3. Mercato di Testaccio (Via Beniamino Franklin, 00118 Roma, Italy, http://www.mercatoditestaccio.it/)

If you are a foodie, this is a market you should visit. Except for buying exceptional food, you can also have your lunch here.

4. Coin (Piazzale Appio, 7, http://www.coin.it/ **)**

The Coin is an upper-middle department store, with interesting Italian fashion, clothes, home décor, and other shops that are usually found in malls.

5. Centro Commerciale Euroma 2 (83 Via dell'Oceano Pacifico)
A shopping mall with high-street brands. Most of the shops have products "made in Italy", such as shoes, clothes, bags, and accessories.

6. Via Sannio Market (Via Sannio)

An outdoor market for clothes, which might be new or old, original or fake. You should always negotiate the price.

7. Mercato Trionfale (3 Via Andrea Doria)
A huge food market in Rome. Here, you will find fish, fruits, vegetables, meat etc. Closed on Saturday and Sunday. Open all the other days from 7 AM to 2 PM.

8. Coin (133 Via Cola di Rienzo)

9. La Feltrinelli (11 Largo Torre Argentina)

Inside the Bookstore of La Feltrinelli (credit)

The most famous bookstore in Italy. A great place for book lovers.

10. Mercato Monti (46 Via Leonina, mercatomonti.com)

This has started as a way for the vendors of Via Monti, to get rid of their overstock and it hosts items from more than 35 different vendors. You will find jewels, vintage clothes, art, clothes and much more. It takes place every Saturday and Sunday.

Our favorite Dining Place in Rome

We have tried many restaurants in Rome. We do not like the ones at Piazza Navona, Piazza di Spagna and close to other touristic places. The food is ok there but compared to the prices you pay, the value for money is not that good. Below you can see the Piazza Navona and its several restaurants and cafeterias.

Piazza Navona (Image Credit, Giuseppe Milo, Flickr/cc)

Moreover, the Aperitivo in Rome is not that great compared to the Aperitivo experience in other places in Italy. If you are not familiar with Aperitivo, in Italy, after 18:00 you can go to a bar, pay 6 to 10 € and enjoy your drink with unlimited buffet dinner (pasta, snacks,). However, in Rome, the aperitivo buffet does not include much food. In some cases, they offer almost nothing – just a couple of snacks. You should try to drink Spritz or Grappa Baricata for an aperitive. We prefer the Grappa more than Spritz.

We enjoyed ourselves at the **Maracuja Restaurant** which is close to Colosseum. It is one of the top-rated restaurants in Tripadvisor as well. We paid 50€ for two persons and had the best Gnocchi and Pasta with Seafood of our lives. Below some screenshots:

1st Day In Rome - Itinerary

9:00
Arrival at the Fiumicino Airport which is 28 km west of the city center

9:30
Take the train *Leonardo Express* to *Roma Termini* station and then take the underground (line A) to *Repubblica*. Accommodate in the hotel.
View *ZoomTip 1*
Cost: 14€ *Leonardo Express*

10:30
Accommodate in the hotel and then visit the *Colosseum* and the *Palatino*.
The *Colosseum* is the main attraction of Rome, and it has become through years its primary symbol (exactly like the *Eiffel Tower* in *Paris*). Nowadays its underground is uncovered, but Italian Government is planning to take it back to its origin. Who knows, maybe in the future it will be used to host concerts or events like the *Verona's Arena*.
Palatino is one of the seven hills of Rome, and it is one of the most ancient and rich of monuments. Nowadays it is an open air gigantic museum.
View *ZoomTip 2.1*

Cost: Ticket 12€. You can buy a Skip-The-Line, Escorted VIP Colosseum Entrance with 21 EUR, here. This is more expensive from the normal ticket but it gets you a fast-track reserved entry at your selected time to the Colosseum, you get escorted inside the Colosseum, Roman Forum, and Palatine and visit them at your own pace and save time from waiting in the long lines. Have a look at the photo below; you will not need to wait in the left or right lines but get directly inside the Colosseum.

13:00

Lunch at *Hostaria Isidoro al Colosseo*
Let's taste here some typical Roman food. For more information view ZoomTip 3 and our detailed guide at the end of this guide, where you will find 15 Roman dishes to try.
Address: Via di San Giovanni in Laterano, 59/A,
http://www.hostariaisidoro.com/
Tel: (+39) 06 700 82 66
Hours: 12:00 to 15:00 and 19:00 to 23:00

14:00

Visit *Roman Forum* - View *ZoomTip 2.1*
Roman Forum is maybe a less famous attraction than Colosseum, but it is one of the most precious millennial monuments you can find in Rome, as it is the cradle of the Occidental society.-(the ticket purchased for the *Colosseum* is valid for this attraction too)

17:30

Visit the *Altar of the Fatherland* - View *ZoomTip 2.1*
The *Altar of the Fatherland* is, as, in other European countries, one of the most important symbols of the Italian

state and it remembers all the soldiers died in recent wars and whose corpses remained without a name and often buried in mass graves. Italian Altar is also a beautiful monument which worths a visit.

19:30
Return to the hotel and have dinner

21:00
Have a night walk through the city, and you will discover that Rome becomes much more beautiful during the evening. It is an unforgettable experience.
If you want to continue your evening out, and you are looking for pubs/bars, keep in mind that there are many places in Pigneto, San Lorenzo, and Trastevere neighborhoods and at the Campo de' Fiori area.

Our recommendations are the **Trinity College Pub**, the **Primo Cafè** (the one in Via Dei Baullari also has an excellent aperitif in the late afternoon) and the **Random Pub.**
Trinity College Pub: Via del Collegio Romano, 6, 00186 Roma RM, http://www.trinity-rome.com/
The Primo Café: Piazza Campo de' Fiori, 6/7, 00186 Roma RM, http://www.primocafe.it/
Random Pub: Via Nomentana Nuova, 103, 00141 Roma RM

You can also choose one of the places that are recommended by the locals, such as:
you can choose one of the following recommendations:
-**Bar Pompi** (7 Via Albalonga)**:** It's a bar, cafeteria, and restaurant, famous for its tiramisu. It has many indoor and outdoor tables.
- **Freni e Frezioni** (*4 Via del Politeama*)**:** This is an excellent choice for an aperitivo, which means that you just pay for the drink and you can choose food from a buffet for free. The aperitivo starts at 7 PM and the cost of the drink is 8 EUR; food is for free as said. It's live and youthful, and it is located Piazza Trilussa in Trastevere.

- **Bar San Calisto** (3 Piazza di San Calisto): Nice people-watching spot. It is a traditional Roman bar where people shout the orders at the back. Here you can also enjoy some home-made ice-cream and a hot chocolate during winter.
- **Salotto 42** (Piazza di Pietra): You can come here after dinner and enjoy a nice glass of wine while looking at the wonderful square and the temple of Adriano.
- **Ma Che Siete Venuti a Fa** (25 Via Di Benedetta): Great collection of beers from all over the world.

If you are looking for **nightclubs,** some choices are:
- **La Cabala** (25 Via de Soldati): It is on the third floor or an ancient building close to Piazza Navona and it is one of the most popular discos in Rome. This might get expensive (e.g. 15 EUR for a drink), so be prepared. *Opening Times:* **Piano bar** 11.30pm-3.30am Tue-Thur; 11.30pm-4.30am Fri, Sat. **Disco** 12.30am-5am Fri, Sat. Both closed June-Aug.

1st Day in Rome - Map

Below you can get the maps that correspond to all the activities that we recommend for your first day in Rome. These maps are accessible in Google Maps format so that you can quickly zoom in/out and use them from your tablet or smartphone when you are in Rome.

Get this map online:
https://www.google.com/maps/d/edit?mid=z4eFn0XnrCGg.kYpwaQnPosf8

ZoomTip 1.1: Transportation in Rome

Rome, as other European capitals, is a quite big city full of attractions, things to do and places where to eat something special. Because of the dimension of the town center and the number of monuments and sites to visit, we suggest you explore it using **public transport services**.

Using the underground you will reach every place in a few minutes avoiding the traffic spending a very few euros. Bus and tram service is slower but allow you to reach every angle of the city without walking more than 500 meters. The three services share the same ticket that you can buy in every underground station of line A and B, every station of the train Roma-Fiumicino and Roma-Viterbo (for a more detailed list you can visit the official local transport site at http://www.atac.roma.it/page.asp?p=21&i=14). Every ticket costs 1.50€/100min; however, we suggest you buy the 48h ticket for 12.50€.

At the end of the guide, you can find the right phrases in Italian to ask for a ticket if the seller does not speak English/your language (that is sorrowfully common in Italy).

If you have an internet connection you can also use the official site to plan your movings (http://viaggiacon.atac.roma.it/).
If at some point, you are too tired to get the public transport you can take a taxi by calling one of the following phone numbers: **063570, 064994, 066645, 068822**. Of course, you can also use the Uber application.

Buses are unpredictable and can come at any point time. There are clear signs with the routes and the lines.

ZoomTip 1.2: Information on the Monuments
Colosseum & Roman forum

The Colosseum (Image Credit: Tim Sackton/Flickr cc)

The Colosseum or Coliseum, also known as the Flavian Amphitheatre or Colosseo is an oval amphitheater in the center of the city of Rome. Built of concrete and sand, it is the largest amphitheater ever built. The Colosseum is situated just east of the Roman Forum. Construction began under emperor Vespasian in AD 72 and was completed in AD 80 under his successor and heir Titus.

Further modifications were made during the reign of Domitian (81–96).[4] These three emperors are known as the Flavian dynasty, and the amphitheater was named in Latin for its association with their family name (Flavius).

The Colosseum could hold, it is estimated, between **50,000** and **80,000** spectators, having an average audience of some 65,000; it was used for gladiatorial contests and public spectacles such as mock sea battles (for only a short time as the hypogeum was soon filled in with mechanisms to support the other activities), animal hunts, executions, re-enactments of famous battles, and dramas based on Classical mythology. The building ceased to be used for entertainment in the early medieval era. It was later reused for such purposes as housing, workshops, quarters for a religious order, a fortress, a quarry, and a Christian shrine.

Although partially ruined because of damage caused by earthquakes and stone-robbers, the Colosseum is still an iconic symbol of Imperial Rome. It is one of Rome's most popular tourist attractions and also has links to the Roman Catholic Church, as each Good Friday the Pope leads a torchlit "Way of the Cross" procession that starts in the area around the Colosseum.

The Colosseum is also depicted on the Italian version of the five-cent euro coin.

The **name Colosseum** has long been believed to be derived from a colossal statue of Nero nearby (the statue of Nero was named after the Colossus of Rhodes). This statue was later remodeled by Nero's successors into the likeness of Helios (Sol) or Apollo, the sun god, by adding the appropriate solar crown. Nero's head was also replaced several times with the heads of succeeding emperors. Despite its pagan links, the statue remained standing well into the medieval era and was credited with magical powers. It came to be seen as an iconic symbol of the permanence of Rome.

In the 8th century, a famous epigram attributed to the Venerable Bede celebrated the symbolic significance of the statue in a prophecy that is variously quoted: *Quamdiu stat Colisæus, stat et Roma; Quando cadet colisæus, cadet et Roma; Quando cadet Roma, cadet et Mundus* ("as long as the Colossus stands, so shall Rome; when the Colossus falls, Rome shall fall; when Rome falls, so falls the world"). This is often mistranslated to refer to the Colosseum rather than the Colossus. However, at the time that the Pseudo-Bede wrote, the masculine noun coliseus was applied to the statue rather than to what was still known as the Flavian amphitheater.

The Colossus did eventually fall, possibly being pulled down to reuse its bronze. By the year 1000, the name "Colosseum" had been coined to refer to the amphitheater. The statue itself was largely forgotten and only its base survives, situated between the Colosseum and the nearby Temple of Venus and Roma. [Source: Wikipedia]

Ticket: 12€, buy it at http://www.coopculture.it/colosseo-e-shop.cfm
Opening hours: 8:30-19:15

Altar of the Fatherland [Altare Della Patria]

Altare Della Patria (Image Credit: Maciek Lulko/Flickr cc)

The **Altare della Patria** ([al'ta:re della 'pa:trja]; English: "Altar of the Fatherland"), also known as the Monumento Nazionale a Vittorio Emanuele II ("National Monument to Victor Emmanuel II") or **Il Vittoriano,** is a monument built in honor of Victor Emmanuel, the first king of a unified Italy, located in Rome, Italy. It occupies a site between the Piazza Venezia and the Capitoline Hill.

The eclectic structure was designed by Giuseppe Sacconi in 1885; sculpture for it was parceled out to established sculptors all over Italy, such as Leonardo Bistolfi and Angelo Zanelli. It was inaugurated in 1911 and completed in 1925.

The Vittoriano features stairways, Corinthian columns, fountains, an equestrian sculpture of Victor Emmanuel and two statues of the goddess Victoria riding on quadrigas. The structure is 135 m (443 ft) wide and 70 m (230 ft) high. If the quadrigae and winged victories are included, the height reaches 81 m (266 ft). It has a total area of 17,000 square meters.

The base of the structure houses the museum of Italian Unification. In 2007, a panoramic lift was added to the structure, allowing visitors to ride up to the roof for 360-degree views of Rome. [Source: Wikipedia]

Ticket: free
Address: Piazza Venezia, 00186 Roma RM, Italy

2nd Day In Rome - Itinerary

9:00

Visit the *Pantheon*
The Pantheon was built in Ancient Rome as a temple consecrated to all the goddess of the past. The Pantheon was built between 118 AD and 128 AD.
View *ZoomTip 2.2*
Cost: Free

11:00

Visit St. Peter Cathedral in Vatican City
St. Peter Cathedral is the largest and most important cathedral of the Christian Catholic religion. On Sunday you can attend the Mass, which is held by the Pope; every week thousands of people come to Rome to take part in this holy ritual. Remember, to take some food and a bottle of water with you because the area gets very crowded.
View *ZoomTip 2.2*
Cost: Ticket 7€

13:00

Lunch at *Trattoria Vaticano Giggi*
Address: Via Catone 10, Angolo Piazza Risorgimento, Roma, Italia
tel. (+39) 06 3973 0551
View *ZoomTip 3*

14:00

Continue the exploration of the Vatican City; visit the Vatican Museums.
Vatican City, as sanctioned by an agreement with Italian state, is an entirely independent State. Vatican Museums are one of the most equipped museums in the world, and it deserves a depth visit.
Cost: Ticket 16€. If you want to buy a Skip-The-Line Vatican Museum with Escorted Entrance, click here. It costs 27 EUR per person and can save you a lot of time from the waiting

lines, as the Vatican Museum is one of the busiest museums in the world.

If you want to get a fast entrance to the Vatican museum, plus a tour to Sistine and St Peters, you can get it for 54 EUR per person here. If you want to get a Skip-The-Line to St. Peter's Top of the Dome, the cost is 31 EUR and you can book it here.

Entrance to the Vatican Museum

18:00
Visit Trevi fountain
Trevi's fountain is a masterpiece of sculpture and engineering. Remember to throw a little coin in the water turned over as tradition.
View *ZoomTip 2.2*

There is a free walking tour of the fountains, squares, churches in Rome, that you can book here.

20:00
Return to the hotel and have dinner
If you want to continue your evening out, and you are looking for pubs/bars, keep in mind that there are many places in Pigneto, San Lorenzo, and Trastevere neighborhoods and Campo de' Fiori area.

Our recommendations are the **Trinity College Pub (Via del Collegio Romano, 6,** http://www.trinity-rome.com/ **)**, the **Primo Cafè** (the one in Via Dei Baullari also has an excellent aperitif in the late afternoon) or you can choose one of the following recommendations:

-**Bar Pompi (**7 Via Albalonga**):** It's a bar, cafeteria, and restaurant, famous for its tiramisu. It has many indoor and outdoor tables.

- **Freni e Frezioni** (*4 Via del Politeama*)**:** This is an excellent choice for an aperitivo, which means that you just pay for the drink and you can choose food from a buffet for free. The aperitivo starts at 7 PM and the cost of the drink is 8 EUR; food is for free as said. It's live and youthful, and it is located Piazza Trilussa in Trastevere.

- **Bar San Calisto (**3 Piazza di San Calisto)**:** Nice people-watching spot. It is a traditional Roman bar where people shout the orders at the back. Here you can also enjoy some home-made ice-cream and a hot chocolate during winter.

- **Salotto 42** (Piazza di Pietra): You can come here after dinner and enjoy a nice glass of wine while looking at the wonderful square and the temple of Adriano.

- **Ma Che Siete Venuti a Fa** (25 Via Di Benedetta): Great collection of beers from all over the world.

If you are looking for nightclubs, some choices are:
- **La Cabala** (25 Via de Soldati): It is on the third floor or an ancient building close to Piazza Navona and it is one of the most popular discos in Rome. This might get expensive (e.g. 15 EUR for a drink), so be prepared. *Opening Times:* ***Piano bar*** 11.30pm-3.30am Tue-Thur; 11.30pm-4.30am Fri, Sat. ***Disco*** 12.30am-5am Fri, Sat. Both closed June-Aug.

La Cabala in Christmas Time

La Cabala View from Inside

- **Piper Club** (9 Via de Tagliamento): This is a night club that opened in 1965. Today, it is a disco and a club with live music or pop, rock and indie style music. Every Friday it plays vintage music from the 70's and 80's. On Saturday it plays modern hits and electronic music and is frequented by a young audience (around 20 years old). Have a look at the photos at https://www.facebook.com/PiperClubRomaOfficialpage/photos/?tab=album&album_id=1143751182369196, so that you don't feel out of your comfort zone if visiting this place.

The Piper Club

If you feel like walking, you can also get a 3 hour evening walking tour of Rome, which costs 25 EUR per person. You can book it here. This might be pretty interesting, as Rome's monuments are very beautiful during the evening. Have a look at the Trevi fountain below as an example.

Fontana Di Trevi During the Evening

2nd Day in Rome – Map

Below you can get the maps that correspond to all the activities that we recommend for your second day in Rome. These maps are accessible in Google Maps format so that you can quickly zoom in/out and use them from your tablet or smartphone when you are in Rome.

Second day in Rome Activities

Get this map online:
https://drive.google.com/open?id=1DIitvJsObHFMNxdvWineqETFbvY&usp=sharing

ZoomTip 2.1: Information on the Monuments

Pantheon

Pantheon in Rome (Image Credit: Ruben Nadador/Flickr cc)

The Pantheon from Greek Πάνθειον meaning "[temple] of every god") is a former Roman temple, now a church, in Rome, Italy, on the site of an earlier temple commissioned by Marcus Agrippa during the reign of Augustus (27 BC – 14 AD). The present building was completed by emperor Hadrian and probably dedicated about 126 AD. He retained Agrippa's original inscription, which has confused its date of construction as the original Pantheon burnt down so it is not certain when the present one was built.

The building is circular with a portico of large granite Corinthian columns (eight in the first rank and two groups of four behind) under a pediment. A rectangular vestibule links the porch to the rotunda, which is under a coffered concrete dome, with a central opening (oculus) to the sky. Almost two thousand years after it was built, the Pantheon's dome is still the world's largest unreinforced concrete dome. The height to the oculus and the diameter of the interior circle are the same, 142 feet (43 m).

It is one of the best-preserved of all Ancient Roman buildings, in large part because it has been in continuous use throughout its history, and since the 7th century, the Pantheon has been used as a church dedicated to "St. Mary and the Martyrs" (Latin: Santa Maria ad Martyres) but informally known as "Santa Maria Rotonda". The square in front of the Pantheon is called **Piazza della Rotonda**.

The Pantheon is a state property; in 2016 it was visited by over 6 million people.

The Pantheon's large circular domed cella, with a conventional temple portico front, was unique in Roman architecture. Nevertheless, it became a standard exemplar when classical styles were revived and has been copied many times by later architects. [Source: Wikipedia]

The impressive dome in Pantheon (Image Credit: Kongprepan/Flickr cc)

Ticket: free
Opening hours: 9:00-19:30, Sun 9:00-18:00
Website: http://www.turismoroma.it/cosa-fare/pantheon
Typical Hours To Spend Here: 45 minutes
Address: Piazza della Rotonda, 00186 Roma RM, Italy

Vatican City

The Vatican City (Image Credit: Polyber49/Flickr cc)

Vatican City is a country located within the city of Rome. With an area of approximately 44 hectares (110 acres) and a population of 1,000, it is the smallest state in the world by both area and population. However, formally it is not sovereign, with sovereignty being held by the Holy See.

It is an ecclesiastical or sacerdotal-monarchical state (a type of theocracy) ruled by the Bishop of Rome – the Pope. The highest state functionaries are all Catholic clergy of various national origins. Since the return of the Popes from Avignon in 1377, they have generally resided at the Apostolic Palace within what is now Vatican City, although at times residing instead in the Quirinal Palace in Rome or elsewhere.

Vatican City is distinct from the Holy See (Latin: Sancta Sedes), which dates back to early Christianity and is the main episcopal see of 1.2 billion Latin and Eastern Catholic adherents around the globe. The independent city-state, on the other hand, came into existence in 1929 by the Lateran Treaty between the Holy See and Italy, which spoke of it as a new creation, not as a vestige of the much larger Papal States (756–1870), which had previously encompassed much of central Italy. According to the terms of the treaty, the Holy

See has "full ownership, exclusive dominion, and sovereign authority and jurisdiction" over the city-state.

Within Vatican City are religious and cultural sites such as St. Peter's Basilica, the Sistine Chapel and the Vatican Museums. They feature some of the world's most famous paintings and sculptures. The unique economy of Vatican City is supported financially by the sale of postage stamps and tourist mementos, fees for admission to museums, and the sale of publications. [Source: Wikipedia]

Ticket: 7€ (cathedral), 16€ (museums). No wait ticket to Vatican Museum, Sistine Chapel, and St Peters costs 57 EUR and you can book it here.

Opening hours: 7:00-19:00 (cathedral), 9:00-18:00 (museum – last admission at 16:00)

St. Peter Cathedral, Vatican Museums

Trevi's fountain

Trevi Fountain (Fontana di Trevi) - [Image Credit: Konprepan/Flickr cc]

The **Trevi Fountain** (Italian: Fontana di Trevi) is a fountain in the Trevi district in Rome, Italy, designed by Italian architect Nicola Salvi and completed by Pietro Bracci. Standing 26.3 meters (86 ft) high and 49.15 meters (161.3 ft) wide, it is the largest Baroque fountain in the city and one of the most famous fountains in the world.

The fountain has appeared in several notable films, including Federico Fellini's La Dolce Vita and the eponymous Three Coins in the Fountain.

Ticket: free

3d Day in Rome – Itinerary

8:30
Check out from the hotel, deposit your luggage and visit *Villa Borghese* and *Galleria Borghese*
Visit a unique gallery in the world: immersed in a beautiful park, it contains masterpieces made by Caravaggio and Bernini.
View *ZoomTip 2.3*
Cost: Ticket 15.5€ plus 5 EUR online booking fee. If you want to pre-reserve your ticket, to skip the lines, the cost is 19 EUR and you can book it here. **Important Notice:** You have to do a pre-booking for a 2-hour time slot and tickets sell out months in advance.
Tour Available: You can get a Skip the Line: Borghese Gallery and Gardens Half-Day Tour, with 50 EUR per person, here.

11:00
Visit *Campidoglio*
Nowadays is Rome town hall but it has a great story to discover hidden inside.
View *ZoomTip 2.3*
Cost: Ticket 15€

13:00
Lunch at *Edoardo II*
Address: Vicolo Margana, 14, Piazza Venezia, Roma, Italia
tel. (+39) 06 6994 2499
View *ZoomTip 3*

14:00
Visit *Piazza di Spagna*
View *ZoomTip 2.3*

15:30
Visit *Piazza Navona*
View *ZoomTip 2.3*

17:00
Take your luggage and go to the airport.
View *ZoomTip 2.3*

3d Day in Rome – Map

Below you can get the maps that correspond to all the activities that we recommend for your third day in Rome. These maps are accessible in Google Maps format so that you can quickly zoom in/out and use them from your tablet or smartphone when you are in Rome.

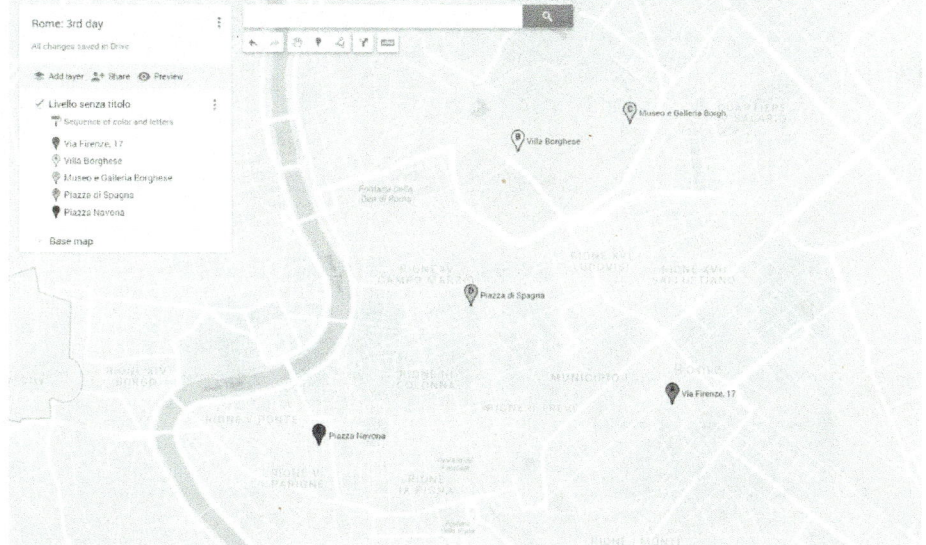

Get this map online:
https://drive.google.com/open?id=1F26XpuIP0KhkuzHNtRZW-3rXNQ0&usp=sharing

ZoomTip 3.1: Information on the Monuments

Villa&Galleria Borghese

Villa Borghese (Image Credit: Jean Dabiera/Flickr cc)

Ticket: 15.5€ plus 5 EUR online booking fee; booking is necessary as there are limited time slots that you can visit this place and tickets can sell out months in advance. Extra visitors will not be accepted at the door without a reservation. Children must also have a reservation and be accompanied by an adult. When you do a pre-booking, you have to print out your reservation and then take it to the basement of Villa Borghese, in order to exchange it for a ticket and leave your belongings and get an audio guide; you will be asked to leave your ID as a guarantee.

You only have two hours to visit the area. Then you have to make room for the new groups. The maximum of people allowed in at any time slot is 360 people. Moreover, you cannot bring a purse or a bag or a backpack inside. If you do, they will give you a plastic bag to place everything inside, and you will have to check it in and get your belongings back upon your exit. There is a long line in which you will have to wait for 15 minutes to check in your plastic bag with your belongings. You can also hire an electric bike to roam around the gardens, for 15 EUR.

If you want to pre-reserve your ticket, to skip the lines, the cost is 19 EUR and you can book it here. If you buy this pre-reserved ticket, go to the ticket counter at the Borghese Gallery to exchange your voucher and redeem your reserved ticket. It is recommended that you do this at least 30 minutes in advance of your reserved time slot.

Opening hours: Tue-Sun 09:00 to 19:00. Admission every 2 hours; last admission at 17:00.

Website: Click Here

Closest Stations: Underground Line A: nearest stop Flaminio or Spagna; Bus n. 116; 88, 95, 490, 495.

Tour Available: You can get a Skip the Line: Borghese Gallery and Gardens Half-Day Tour, with 50 EUR per person, here.

Campidoglio (Image Credit: Robert Bolton, Flickr cc)

The Capitoline Hill between the Forum and the Campus Martius is one of the Seven Hills of Rome.
The hill was earlier known as Mons Saturnius, dedicated to the god Saturn. The word Capitolium first meant the temple of Jupiter Optimus Maximus later built here, and afterward it was used for the whole hill (and even other temples of Jupiter on other hills), thus Mons Capitolinus (the adjective noun of Capitolium). Ancient sources refer the name to caput ("head", "summit") and the tale was that when laying the foundations of the temple, the head of a man was found. Some sources even saying it was the head of some Tolus or Olus. The Capitolium was regarded by the Romans as indestructible and was adopted as a symbol of eternity.
By the 16th century, Capitolinus had become Capitolino in Italian, and Capitolium Campidoglio. The Capitoline Hill contains few ancient ground-level ruins, as they are almost entirely covered up by Medieval and Renaissance palaces (now housing the Capitoline Museums) that surround a piazza, a significant urban plan designed by Michelangelo.
Influenced by Roman architecture and Roman republican times, the word Capitolium still lives in the English word capitol. The Capitol Hill in Washington, D.C. is widely

assumed to be named after the Capitoline Hill, but the relation is not clear. [Source: Wikipedia]
Ticket: 15€
Opening hours: 9:30-19:30
Website: http://en.museicapitolini.org/

Piazza di Spagna & Piazza Navona

Piazza Di Spagna (Image Credit: Paolo Fefe/Flickr cc)

Piazza di Spagna, at the bottom of the Spanish Steps, is one of the most famous squares in Rome. It owes its name to the Palazzo di Spagna, the seat of the Embassy of Spain among the Holy See. Nearby is the famed Column of the Immaculate Conception of the Blessed Virgin Mary.
In the middle of the square is the famous Fontana della Barcaccia, dating to the beginning of the baroque period, sculpted by Pietro Bernini and his son, the more famous Gian Lorenzo Bernini.
At the right corner of the Spanish Steps rises the house of the English poet John Keats, who lived there until his death in 1821: nowadays it has been changed into a museum dedicated to him and his friend Percy Bysshe Shelley, displaying books and memorabilia of English romanticism. At the left corner, there is the Babington's tea room, founded in 1893.
The side near Via Frattina is overlooked by the two façades (the main one, designed by Gian Lorenzo Bernini, and the side one created by

Francesco Borromini) of the Palazzo di Propaganda Fide, a property of the Holy See. In front of it, actually in a lengthening of Piazza di Spagna named Piazza Mignanelli, rises the Column of the Immaculate Conception, erected in 1856, two years after the proclamation of the dogma.

The imposing 135-step staircase was inaugurated by Pope Benedict XIII during the 1725 Jubilee; it was released (thanks to French loans granted in 1721–1725) in order to connect the Bourbon Spanish embassy (from which the square takes its name) to the Church of Trinità dei Monti.

It was designed by Alessandro Specchi and Francesco De Sanctis after generations of long and glowing discussions about how to urbanize the steep slope on the side of the Pincian Hill in order to connect it to the church. The final key was the one proposed by Francesco De Sanctis: a great staircase decorated with many garden-terraces, splendidly adorned with flowers in spring and summer. The sumptuous, aristocratic staircase, at the summit of a straight sequence of streets leading down to the Tiber, was designed so that the scenic effects increase more and more while approaching to it. In effect, the creation of long, deep perspectives culminating in monumental wings or backdrops was typical of the great baroque architecture. The Spanish Steps were restored in 1995. [Source: Wikipedia]

Piazza Navona (Image Credit: Giuseppe Milo/Flickr cc)

Piazza Navona (pronounced [ˈpjattsa naˈvoːna]) is built on the site of the Stadium of Domitian, built in the 1st century AD, and follows the form of the open space of the stadium. The ancient Romans went there to watch the agones ("games"), and hence it was known as "Circus Agonalis" ("competition arena"). It is believed that over time the name changed to in avone to navone and eventually to Navona.

Defined as a public space in the last years of 15th century, when the city market was transferred there from the Campidoglio, Piazza Navona was transformed into a highly significant example of Baroque Roman architecture and art during the pontificate of Innocent X, who reigned from 1644 until 1655, and whose family palace, the Palazzo Pamphili, faced the Piazza. It features important sculptural and creations: in the center stands the famous Fontana dei Quattro Fiumi or Fountain of the Four Rivers (1651) by Gian Lorenzo Bernini, topped by the Obelisk of Domitian, brought in pieces from the Circus of Maxentius;[2] the church of Sant'Agnese in Agone by Francesco Borromini, Girolamo Rainaldi, Carlo Rainaldi and others; and the aforementioned Pamphili palace, also by Girolamo Rainaldi, that accommodates the long gallery designed by Borromini and frescoed by Pietro da Cortona.

Piazza Navona has two other fountains. At the southern end is the Fontana del Moro with a basin and four Tritons sculpted by Giacomo della Porta (1575) to which, in 1673, Bernini added a statue of a Moor, or a North African Muslim, wrestling with a dolphin. At the northern end is the Fountain of Neptune (1574) also created by Giacomo della Porta; the statue of Neptune, by Antonio Della Bitta, was added in 1878 to create a balance with La Fontana del Moro.

During its history, the piazza has hosted theatrical events and other ephemeral activities. From 1652 until 1866, when the festival was suppressed, it was flooded on every Saturday and Sunday in August in elaborate celebrations of the Pamphilj family. The pavement level was raised in the 19th century, and in 1869 the market was moved to the nearby Campo de' Fiori. A Christmas market is held in the Piazza. [Source: Wikipedia]

Ticket: free

Where to Eat in Rome

We have compiled a list of the best places to eat in under consideration a medium budget and the loca of Italians. We will not guide you through the more restaurants in Rome, as these are easy to find and excellent. We will help you discover the best value for money restaurants to try the local delicacies.

#1 Necci *(68 Via Fanfulla da Lodi, http://www.necci1924.com, open every day from 8 am until 1 am)*

This is a place that serves breakfast, lunch, aperitif, and dinner and is open from 8 am until 2 am. It serves a great aperitif every day, except Sunday, at 7 pm, with a nice selection of food. It has a beautiful garden where you can enjoy a glass of wine or a coffee and you will find many parents with kids playing around. Pasolini is a famous Italian screenwriter and movie director, who was coming to Necci all the time, so this has added a lot to the fame of this place. It is in the area of Pigneto and is frequented by hipsters. Try the appetizers and particularly the *Polpette di Melanzane and Fiori di Zucca*. The burgers cost 12€ and the main courses 14€. In the morning, it's a very cheap place for a cappuccino (1€), an Italian croissant called "cornetto" (1€) or a cornetto with ham and cheese (2.5€). The staff is very friendly and will make you feel like home. It's peak hours are 10 pm to 11 pm.

2 Dar Poeta (45 Vicolo del Bologna, http://www.darpoeta.com, open every day from 12 pm to 12 am, tel +39 06 588 0516)

This is a restaurant in Trastevere and close to the Piazza Santa Maria. You come here for the pizza, which is prepared for you in a wood oven. It is always packed with people and it's not a quiet place. You should get the Nutella/ricotta calzone as a dessert. Dar Poeta is considered to be one of the best pizzerias in central Rome. The peak hours here are from 8 pm to 10 pm and if you haven't booked a table you may have to wait up to 30 minutes to be seated. The service is typical, without a lot of conversations, especially during the peak times and some visitors may even find it unfriendly, so be prepared for that. The atmosphere here is not something special though but we told you that you come here for the pizza and the fair price. For two pizzas and a liter of wine (which is always served cold unless you ask for a room temperatured wine), you should expect to pay around 28€. The carbonara pizza is one of their favorites and if you like spicy food, get the "Dar Poeta" pizza. Dar Poeta restaurant doesn't serve pasta and it doesn't have any wi-fi for its visitors.

#3 **Da Baffetto** (114 Via del Governo Vecchio, open every day from 12 pm to 15:30 pm and 18:30 to 1 am, http://www.pizzeriabaffetto.it/)

An amazing pizzeria close to the Piazza Navona, which serves a thin and tasteful Roman pizza and Calzone. The peak hours here are from 19:00 to 22:00. If you come here after 8 pm you may have to wait in the queue to be seated. It's a legendary pizzeria in Rome. You can access the menu in English at http://www.pizzeriabaffetto.it/menu-ing/.
Unfortunately, this is a first-come first-served pizzeria and you cannot reserve a table.

#4 **Porto Fluviale** (22 Via del Porto Fluviale, open every day from 12:30 pm to 2 am, http://www.portofluviale.com/)

An industrial style restaurant with a Nordic design, which is open from the morning till the evening and it serves different main courses, such as meat, pasta, vegetables, salads, and pizza. You should better make a booking before you go, as it is very popular. They also offer a lunch buffet, which is great and is much cheaper on the weekdays than during the weekends. The staff is very friendly and speaks great English.

The peak hours here are from 21:00 to 23:00 and a suggestion would be to come here for an aperitif and then get a pizza, a couple of drinks and enjoy the atmosphere.

#5 Bar Del Fico (26 Piazza del Fico, open every day from 8 am until 2 am, http://www.bardelfico.com/en)

This is mainly a bar, which also serves lunch, near Piazza Navona. You can have a breakfast, lunch or dinner here. It's a crowdy and noisy place, with loud music and a lot of people sitting outside of it when the weather is good. It's a place that is more fun in the summer than during the winter. The best suggestions here are the wood-oven cooked pizza, the burgers, and the steaks. It offers free wi-fi, though it doesn't work always well. The peak hours here are from 22:00 to 12:00 am

#6 La Montecarlo (13 Vicolo Savelli, everyday 12 pm to 01 am http://www.lamontecarlo.it/)

A great restaurant, preferred by many locals which serves excellent pizza, pasta, meat, and suppli. As it is not a touristic place, you have to try your Italian a little bit when ordering or trying to communicate with the waiters.

#7 Il Sorpasso (31 Via Properzio, every day from 07:30 to 1:00 am, Saturday from 9 am to 1 am, http://sorpasso.info/)

A place with a great ambiance, where you can try Italian food, wine, cheese, ham, prosciutto, and several different cocktails. It's a trendy place, which is also an excellent choice for an aperitif.

#8 La Zanzara (84 Via Crescenzio, every day from 8 am to 2 am, http://www.lazanzararoma.com)

La Zanzara means "the mosquito" in Italian and this is a place that you can go to after your visit to the Vatican City. The best choice would be to come here for an aperitif and you should get here before 6.30 pm as it is difficult to find a table. It's not a touristic place and is frequented usually by Italians. It's not a cheap place though. You can access the menu in English at http://www.lazanzararoma.com/wp-content/uploads/2017/06/INTERNET_MENU_ITA_13_06_2016.pdf.

#9 Pizzarium (43 Via della Meloria, every day from 11 am to 10 pm, http://www.bonci.it)

Pizzarium serves some of the best pizza in Rome. Unfortunately, you cannot get a table here and it offers only pizza by the slice. The materials of the pizza are excellent and the dough is made from organic flour. Gabriele Bonci is the owner.

Where to Find the Best Ice Cream (Gelato) in Rome

The best places to taste the delicious Italian ice cream in Rome are listed below. You can also click on the map to view the Online Google maps and navigate quickly to any one of these:

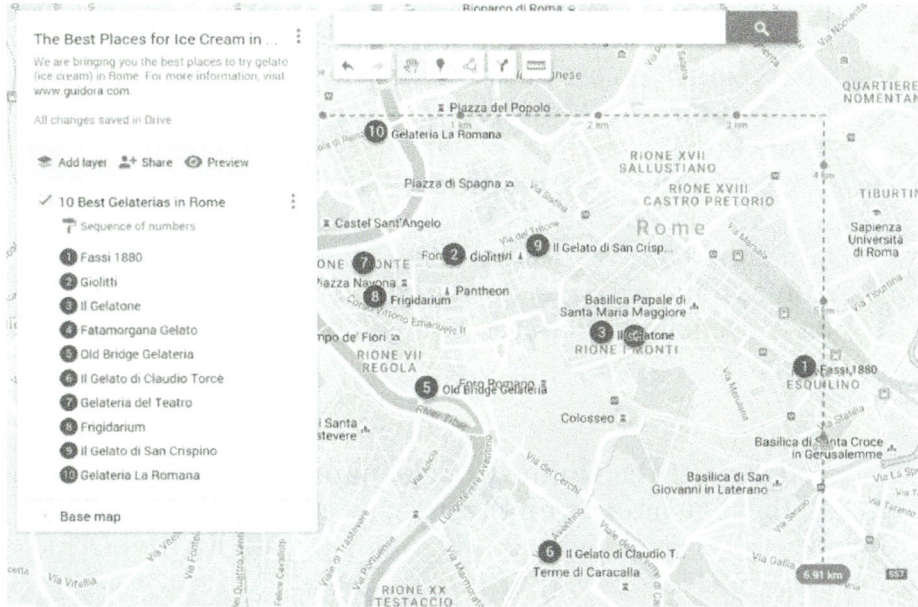

- **Il Palazzo del Freddo di Giovanni Fassi (Gelateria Fassi)-** Via Principe Eugenio 65, Vittorio Emanuele A Line underground station. *www.palazzodelfreddo.it*
- **Giolitti** - via Uffici del Vicario 40, near Montecitorio, the Italian Parliament, and Pantheon. An old shop which operates in Rome for 26 years. Even the daughters of President Obama spent a whole afternoon here during the G8 summit in 2009. *http://www.giolitti.it/*
- **Il Gelatone** - Via Dei Serpenti 28, Monti. They have soy options, which are great for vegans. - http://www.tripadvisor.it/Restau...
- **Fatamorgana:** A different style of ice cream than the regular one you try at most places. Fatamorgana, Rome

- **Old Bridge Gelateria** – Quite popular place, so you may have to wait in a queue. Old Bridge Gelateria, Rome
- **Il Gelato by Claudio Torce.** Close to Via del Corso. Http://hvandenbergh.com/2011/07/.
- **Gelateria del Teatro-** Via de Dan Simone, near Piazza Navona. Try the chocolate with orange, the raspberry and the lavender with lemon.
- **La Gelateria Frigidarium** – via del Governo Vecchio, near Piazza Navona. They use natural ingredients, and you will understand this from the color of the pistachio which is not the one you are used to. Try the raspberry flavor and the fruit flavors. Their chocolates are a bit too sweet, however.
- **Il Gelato di San Crispino** – Via Della Panetteria, near the Trevi Fountain. Try the honey flavor.
- **Gelateria La Romana** - Via Cola di Rienzo, 2, 00193 Roma, Italy, www.gelateriaromana.com, +39 06 3260 9251. Delicious gelateria. You will have to queue in long lines.

You can get the Online Google maps we created for you, with all these Gelaterias on the map, by clicking at: https://drive.google.com/open?id=1lYo8YjltadI3hCUoGsqDGVnrbZc&usp=sharing

Where to Find the Best Pizza in Rome

The best places to taste the delicious Italian pizza in Rome are listed below. You can also click on the map to view the Online Google maps and navigate quickly to any one of these. Please notice that there are two different kind of pizza places in Rome: **"Pizza al taglio,"** which serves the square pieces of pizza that you just grab and go and **"Pizza by the Plate"** which is more like a pizza restaurant.

Click on the maps or at:

https://drive.google.com/open?id=1EyDjKepwaFzdROu4lR2ckdMc00A&usp=sharing to get the online maps in Google maps format.

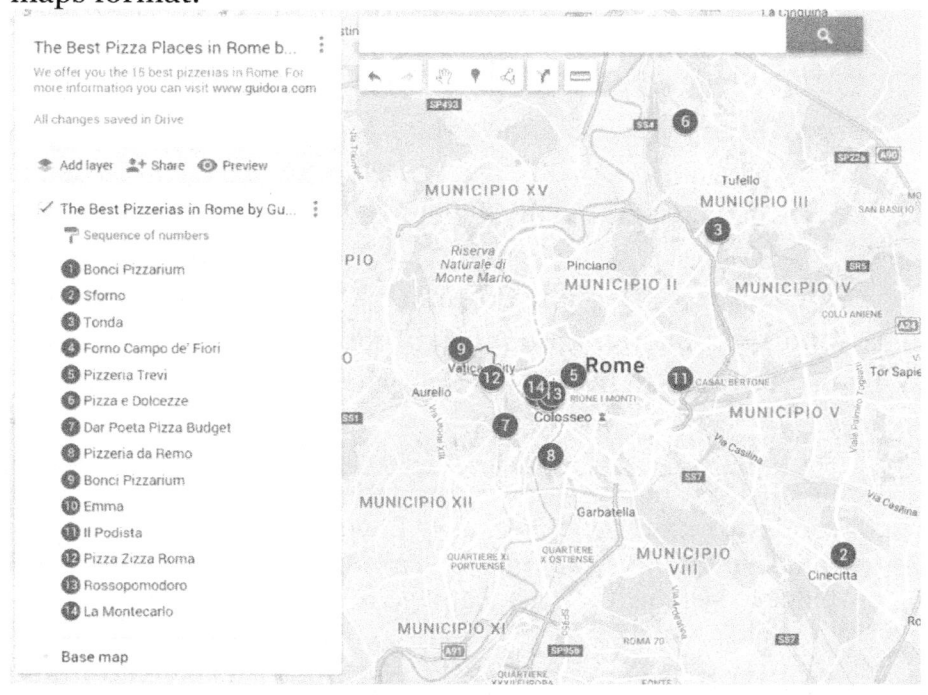

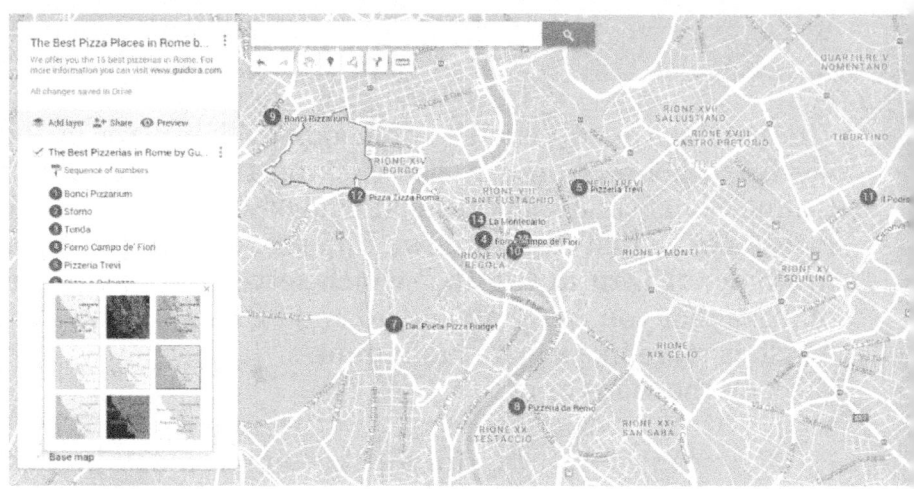

#1 Gabriele Bonci's Pizzarium - Via Della Meloria, 43, 00136 Roma, Italy, www.bonci.it

#2 Sforno – Via Statilio Ottato, 110/116, 00175 Roma, www.sforno.it, +39 06 7154 6118. It offers excellent Neapolitan-style pizza. Operated by Stefano Callegari.

#3 Tonda – Via Valle Corteno, 31, 00141 Roma, +39 06 818 0960. Similar to Sforno, Tonda offers excellent Neapolitan-style pizza. Operated by Stefano Callegari.

#4 Forno Campo de' Fiori, Rome – Piazza Campo Dè Fiori, 22, 00186 Roma. Serves pizzas with a thin and crispy crust. You order by weight, and you select how to have your pizza cut, e.g. in many small pieces so that you can share easily. You will not find a place to seat as it is a grab and go.

#5 Pizzeria Trevi di Paoli Cristian. Via Delle Muratte, 14, 00187 Roma, +39 06 678 5575. It is in the middle of the touristic area of Rome. Here, nine out of ten pizza places are below average, and this place is one of the few exceptions. It is a tiny place, but it offers many choices for fresh pizza.

#6 Pizza e Dolcezze. Via Pian di Scò, 56, 00139 Roma. www.pizzaedolcezze.it. Excellent pizza, desserts and craft beers.

#7 Dar Poeta, Roma - Trastevere - Ristorante Recensioni, Numero di Telefono & Foto - TripAdvisor. **00152,** Piazzale Aurelio, 7, 00152 Roma, darpoeta.com
This is a tiny place with excellent pizza. However, don't order any salads or desserts here as they are of average quality. Stick with the pizza. A small selection of beers and wine too.

#7 Da Remo. Piazza di Santa Maria Liberatrice, 44, 00153 Roma. +39 06 574 6270

#8 Bonci Pizzarium. Via Della Meloria, 43, 00136 Roma. www.bonci.It offers pizza al taglio.

#8 Emma. Via del Monte Della Farina, 28, 00186 Roma. ww.emmapizzeria.com It is located near Largo Torre Argentina. A nice choice if you in the historic center. Stylish place with friendly service.

#9 Il Podista. Via Tiburtina, 224, 00185 Roma,+39 06 4470 0967. It is located in San Lorenzo. If offers delicious and cheap pizza. Frequented mostly by locals.

#10 Pizza Zizza, Via Delle Fornaci, 11, 00100 Roma, next to Saint Peter Square. Right in between Saint Peter square and San Pietro Train Station. Pizza Zizza serves some of the best pizza al taglio in Rome. It is a small place with a couple of tables inside and outside. The ingredients of the Pizza are fresh, and the dough of the pizza matures in a 72 hours period.

#11 Rosso Pomodoro. Largo di Torre Argentina, 1, 00186 Roma, web.rossopomodoro.it, +39 06 6889 2440. In Largo di Torre Argentina, in the city center. It serves excellent Neapolitanean Pizza. Fresh ingredients and excellent pizza dough.
 # 12 La Montecarlo. Vicolo Savelli, 13, 00130 Roma, www.lamontecarlo.it, +39 06 6860 0278. It is located near Piazza Navona.

What Italian dishes to Try Except for Pizza and Pasta

One of the best things about being in Rome is that you can try all the delicious Italian food, such as pasta, pizzas and typical Roman dishes. Here is a guide with the best dishes to try while in Rome.

Pasta Alla Carbonara

Carbonara is an Italian pasta dish from Rome based on eggs, cheese (Pecorino Romano or Parmigiano-Reggiano), bacon (guanciale or pancetta), and black pepper. The pasta is usually spaghetti. However, the Italians also use fettuccine, rigatoni, linguine or bucatini.

Pasta all' amatriciana

Sugo all'amatriciana (Italian pronunciation: [amatri'tʃaːna]) or all amatriciana (in Romanesco dialect) is a traditional Italian pasta sauce based on guanciale (cured pork cheek), pecorino cheese, and tomato. (from Wikipedia)

Italy is the king of the world when it comes to pizza and pasta. However, the Roman culinary experience provides much more than these two obvious choices. Here is a list of the best Roman dishes to try while you are in Rome.

#1 Rosette: This is a bread prepared with a traditional Roman way.

#2 Carciofi Alla Romana (Roman Artichokes): Romans eat only the heart of the artichokes. They usually prepare them on steam, or you can get them fried.

#3 Porchetta: This is pork meat which is roasted together with garlic, rosemary, and fennel. You can also get a sandwich with Porchetta in many places around Rome.

#4 Cervello: This is a more unusual dish, which is calf brains. It is served fried.

#5 Zucchini Flowers: You can get them on a pizza or taste them fried and filled with ricotta cheese. Sometimes you can get them stuffed with smoked salmon.

#6 Suppli: fried rice balls

#7 Saltimbocca Alla Romana: This is veal which is cooked with prosciutto and sage – a little bit of white wine is also used during the cooking process.

#8 Broccoletti Ripassati: This is broccoli cooked with oil, garlic, and chili.

#9 Carpaccio di Spigola: Spigola is the Italian name for Sea Bass. This plate is a must go in Rome, and you should give it a try.

#10 Carpaccio di Pesce Spada: Pesce Spada is the Italian name for the Swordfish. Another fantastic dish that you should try for sure.

#11 Zuppa di Mare: This is a soup prepared with different fruits of the sea.

#12 Sfogliatelli: It is a usually a shell-shaped filled Italian pastry which originates from Napoli and has more than 400 years of history.

#13 Panna Cotta: This is a sweet with thick and sweet cream, which gets its aromas from rum or coffee.

#14 Tiramisu: This is a sweet and the best place to taste it is at "Pompi." There are various "Pompi" in Rome – one is just in front of the Spanish Steps, the biggest one is at Re di Roma metro station and the 3d one is on Via Marconi.

Below you can get the google maps with all the locations of Pompi shops in Rome. For easy navigation, you can also click on
https://drive.google.com/open?id=1zLOiyV6pU6rvULqAaBOLE9s0QVk&usp=sharing

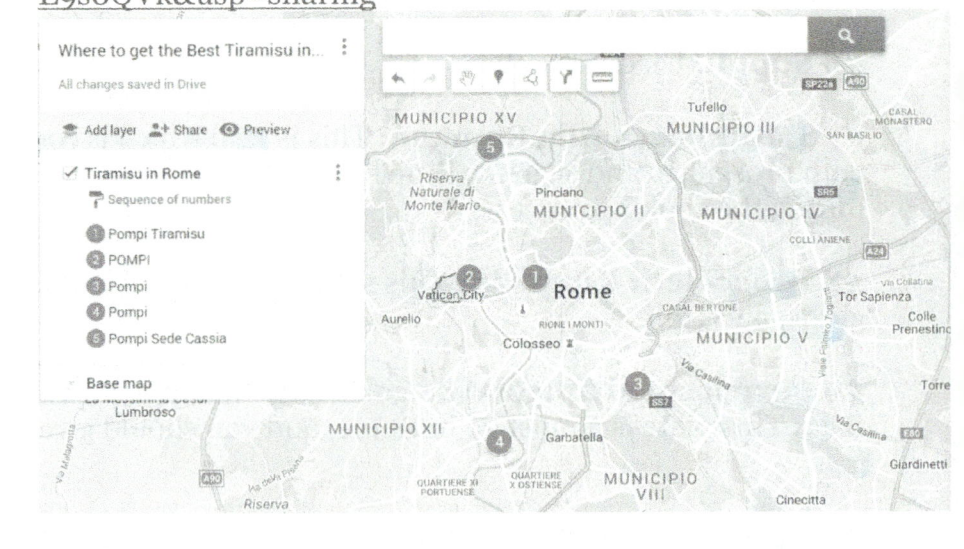

Useful Italian Phrases

Italians who deal with tourism, usually speak some English on a rather comprehensible communication level. However, it is recommended that you learn some Italian Words before you head to Italy.

Common Greetings in Italian

Italian Word	How it is Pronounced in Italian	Meaning
Buongiorno	Bon – jor- no	Goodmorning
Arrivederci	Ar – ree -ve – der- see	Goodbye
Ciao	Ts- a- o	Hi and Goodbye (informal)
Buonasera	Bou- ona- se -ra	Good afternoon. Good Evening.
Buonanotte	Bou-ona-no-te	Good night
Come si chiama?	Ko-me-see-kee-a-ma	What is your name? (formal)
Come ti chiami?	Ko-me-tee-kee- a-mee	What is your name? (informal)
Mi chiamo ...	Mee-kee-a-mo	My name is...
Come sta?	Ko-me-sta	How are you? (formal)
Come stai?	Ko-me-sta-ee	How are you? (informal)
Bene, Grazie	Be-ne-gra-tsee-eh	Fine, thank you

Courtesy Phrases

Italian Word	How it is Pronounced in Italian	Meaning
Per Favore	Per- fa- vo- re	Please
Grazie	Gra- zee- eh	Thank you
Prego	Preh-goh	You are welcome. (It also means, "please, after you").

Mi scusi	Mee-skoo-zee	Excuse me (formal)
Mi dispiace	Mee-dees-pyah-cheh	I am sorry
Scusa	Skoo-za	I am sorry (or excuse me). (informal)
Si	See	yes
No	No	No

Practical Question Words in Italian

Italian Word	How it is Pronounced in Italian	Meaning
Parla Inglese?	Pahr-lah-een-gleh-zeh	Do you speak English?
Chi?	Kee?	Who?
Cosa?	Koh-sah	What?
Quando?	Koo-an-do	When?
Dove?	Doh-veh	Where?
Perche?	Per-keh?	Why?
Come?	Koh-meh	How?
Quanto?	Koo-an-to	How much?

Some of the phrases you may need are:
Scusi, Dov'è la stazione? - Excuse me, where is the station?
Scusi, dov'è il bagno? - Excuse me, where is the bathroom?
Scusi, quanto dista il Piazzale Roma? Excuse me, how far is Piazzale Roma?
Scusi, come si arriva in Piazzale Roma? – Excuse me, how can I get to the Piazzale Roma?

Days of the Week in Italian

Italian Word	How it is Pronounced in Italian	Meaning
Domenica (Do)	Doh-meh-nee-kah	Sunday
Lunedi (Lun)	Loo-neh-dee	Monday
Martedi (Mar)	Mar- teh- dee	Tuesday
Mercoledi (Mer)	Mehr-ko-leh-dee	Wednesday
Giovedi (Gio)	Joh-veh-dee	Thursday

Venerdi (Ven)	Veh-neh-rdee	Friday
Sabato (sab)	Sah-bah-toh	Saturday
Oggi	Oh-jee	Today
Domani	Doh-mah-nee	Tomorrow
Dopodomani	Doh-poh-doh-mah-nee	Day after tomorrow
Ieri	Yeh-ree	yesterday

The Numbers in Italian

1	*uno*	OO-noh
2	*due*	DOO-eh
3	*tre*	TREH
4	*quattro*	KWAHT-troh
5	*cinque*	CHEEN-kweh
6	*sei*	SEH-ee
7	*sette*	SET-teh
8	*otto*	OHT-toh
9	*nove*	NOH-veh
10	*dieci*	dee-EH-chee
11	*undici*	OON-dee-chee
12	*dodici*	DOH-dee-chee
13	*tredici*	TREH-dee-chee
14	*quattordici*	kwaht-TOR-dee-chee
15	*quindici*	KWEEN-dee-chee
16	*sedici*	SEH-dee-chee
17	*diciassette*	dee-chahs-SET-teh
18	*diciotto*	dee-CHOHT-toh
19	*diciannove*	dee-chahn-NOH-veh
20	*venti*	VEN-tee
21	*ventuno*	ven-TOO-noh
22	*ventidue*	ven-tee-DOO-eh
23	*ventitré*	ven-tee-TREH
24	*ventiquattro*	ven-tee-KWAHT-troh
25	*venticinque*	ven-tee-CHEEN-kweh
26	*ventisei*	ven-tee-SEH-ee
27	*ventisette*	ven-tee-SET-teh
28	*ventotto*	ven-TOHT-toh
29	*ventinove*	ven-tee-NOH-veh
30	*trenta*	TREN-tah
40	*quaranta*	kwah-RAHN-tah
50	*cinquanta*	cheen-KWAHN-tah
60	*sessanta*	ses-SAHN-tah
70	*settanta*	set-TAHN-ta
80	*ottanta*	oht-TAHN-ta

90	*novanta*	noh-VAHN-tah
100	*cento*	CHEN-toh

How to Order Food in Italian

Italian Word	How it is Pronouncsssseed in Italian	Meaning
Un cappuccino per favore	Oon-ka-poo-tsee-no per-fa-voh-reh	One cappuccino coffee please.
Di aqua minerale per favore.	Dee a-koo-a mee-neh-rah-leh per fa-voh-reh	Some mineral water please.
Mezzo litro d'acqua, per favore	Meh-zoh lee-tro dah-koo- ah	(When you are thirsty and you want to buy a small bottle of water from a shop on the street): Half a liter of water, please.
Quanto viene?	Koo-an-to vee-en-neh	How much does it cost?
Un gelato, per favore	Oon geh-lah-to per fah-voh-re	One ice cream please
Ci fa il conto, per favore?	Chee- fah eel kon-toh per fa-vo-reh	Could you please bring us the bill?
Vuole l'antipasto?	Voo-o-leh lan-tee-pah-stoh	Would you like an appetizer?
Cosa vorrebbe ordinare?	Koh-sah voh-rebbeh or-dee-nah-reh	What would you like to order?
Ha già deciso?	A tzeea deh-tsee-soh	Have you decided (what to order)?
Cosa Desidera?	Koh-sah deh-see-	What would

	deh-rah	you like?
Cosa desidera ordinare/mangiare?	Koh-sah deh-see-deh-rah or-dee-nah-reh/man-tzah-reh	What would you like to order/eat?
Un momento per favore	Oon moh-mento per fah-voh-reh	One moment please
Non lo so ancora	Non loh soh an-koh-rah	I don't know it yet
Cosa mi può raccomandare?	Koh-sah mee poo-oh rah-koh-men-dah-reh	What could you recommend me?
Qual'è la specialià del giorno?	Koo-al eh lah spe-tseealiah del tzee-o-rnoh	What is the daily special?
Il dolce	Eel doh-l-tseh	The dessert
Il contorno	Eel kon-tor-noh	The side dish
La zuppa	La zoo-pah	Soup
L'insalata	L een-sa-lah-tah	Salad
La salsa	Lah sal-sa	sauce
La verdure	La ver-doo-reh	vegetables
La patate	Lah pa-ta-teh	potatoes
Il riso	Eel ree-so	rice
La carne	La ka-rneh	meat
La pasta	La pasta	pasta
Il maiale	Il ma-ee-a-leh	pork
Il pollo	Eel po-loh	chicken
Il manzo	Eel man-zoh	beef
L'acqua minerale	L a-koo-a mee-neh-rah-leh	Mineral water
Il succo di frutta	Eel soo-koh dee froo-tah	juice
La birra	La bee-rah	Beer
Il vino rosso	Eel vee-noh roh-soh	Red wine
Il vino bianco	Eel vee-noh bee-an-koh	White wine
Lo spumante	Lo spoo-man-teh	bubbly
Lo champagne	Lo sah-mpa-kneh	champagne
L'antipasto	Lan-tee-pa-stoh	starter
Il primo	Eel pree-mo	First course
Il secondo	Eel se-kon-doh	Second course

		(main course)
Io prendo...	ee-o pre-ndoh	I'll have...
Io vorrei	ee-o voh-reh-ee	I would like...
Il conto per favore	Eel ko-ntoh per fa-voh-reh	Could I have the bill please?
Vorrei pagare per favore	Vo-reh-ee pa-gah-reh per fa-voh-reh	I would like to pay please.
La mancia	La man-tsee-a	tip

Thank You!

Thank you for choosing this Guidora guide to Rome. We hope that it is going to help you to make the most out of your stay in Rome.

If you have any feedback on how to improve, or if you just had a great time in Rome and you would like to share that, just send us an email to admin@guidora.com.

Have an amazing time in Rome!

Your friends at Guidora.

Copyright Notice
Guidora Rome in 3 Days Travel Guide ©

All rights reserved. No part of either publication may be reproduced in any material form, including electronic means, without the prior written permission of the copyright owner.

Text and all materials are protected by UK and international copyright and/or trademark law and may not be reproduced in any form except for non-commercial private viewing or with prior written consent from the publisher, with the exception that permission is hereby granted for the use of this material in the form of brief passages in reviews when the source of the quotations is acknowledged.

Disclaimer

The publishers have checked the information in this travel guide, but its accuracy is not warranted or guaranteed. Rome visitors are advised that opening times should always be checked before making a journey.

Tracing Copyright Owners

Every effort has been made to trace the copyright holders of referred material. Where these efforts have not been successful, copyright owners are invited to contact the Editor (Guidora) so that their copyright can be acknowledged and/or the material removed from the publication.

Creative Commons Content

We are most grateful to publishers of Creative Commons material, including images. Our policies concerning this material are (1) to credit the copyright owner, and provide a link where possible (2) to remove Creative Commons material, at once, if the copyright owner so requests - for example, if the owner changes the licensing of an image.

We will also keep our interpretation of the Creative Commons Non-Commercial license under review. Along with, we believe, most web publishers, our current view is that acceptance of the 'Non-Commercial' condition means (1) we must not sell the image or any publication containing the image (2) we may, however, use an image as an illustration for some information which is not being sold or offered for sale.

Note to other copyright owners

We are grateful to those copyright owners who have given permission for their material to be used. Some of the material comes from secondary and tertiary sources. In every case, we have tried to locate the original author or photographer and make the appropriate acknowledgment. In some cases, the sources have proved obscure and we have been unable to track them down. In these cases, we would like to hear from the copyright owners and will be pleased to acknowledge them in future editions or remove the material.

Printed in Great Britain
by Amazon